Henry IV
(Enrico IV)

By

Luigi Pirandello

A New English Version
By
Royston Coppenger

About the Author

Luigi Pirandello was born in Sicily in 1867 to an upper-class family. Pirandello studied Law and Letters, first at the University of Palermo, then at the University of Rome. After a conflict with a Latin professor Pirandello was forced to leave Rome and complete his studies at the University of Bonn, receiving his Doctorate in Romance Philology in 1891. From 1893 to 1903 Pirandello wrote plays, short stories, poems and novels; after the collapse of his father's sulpphur mining business in 1903 Pirandello initially made his living as a teacher. In 1904 his novel *The Late Mattia Pascal* brought him a resounding critical success. His most famous play, *Six Characters in Search of an Author*, was a failure upon its first production in Rome in 1921, but succeeded in Milan a year later. 1922 also saw the first production of Pirandello's *Enrico IV (Henry IV)*. A string of successful novels, plays and story collections followed. Pirandello was awarded the Nobel Prize in Literature in 1934.

Pirandello was an early and enthusiastic supporter of the Italian fascist movement led by Benito Mussolini. Although his relationship to the fascists was fraught with mutual suspicion he remained close to Mussolini and in 1935 donated his Nobel Prize to the Fascist government to be melted down as part of the *Oro alla Patria* ("Gold to the Fatherland") campaign during Mussolini's invasion of Ethiopia. Pirandello died in Rome in 1936.

About the Translation

Pirandello's *Enrico IV* was written in 1922; In his book *Naked masks*, eric Bentley described Pirandello's prose style as

> "Always extremely simple . . . the language of these
> plays is agile, astute, mobile, full of sap,
> bursting with inner vitality; the dialogue, restrained,
> exact, with no ornamental appendages, the images
> immediate and germane, bends itself wonderfully to
> follow the sinuosities of psychological processes."

Regrettably, British author Edward Storer's 1923 translation – still in print and still widely available in a number of editions – adheres much too closely to the complex sentence structure and grammar of the original Italian. In addition, Storer's translations are closely related to the best "modern" British playwrights of the 1920s. Writers like Galsworthy, Priestley, and Lonsdale wrote in a prolix, emotionally formal style that no longer sounds modern to our ears. As a result, the most commonly-used translations of Pirandello's plays maintain an early twentieth-century British diction. Combine this with Storer's often literal translation of Italian sentence structure, and most readers will experience *Henry IV* as a somewhat stiff, sometimes frankly incomprehensible series of overly polite drawing-room colloquies. This is nothing like the muscular, vibrant and direct language described by Bentley.

Tom Stoppard's 2004 version of the play goes a long way towards imbuing Pirandello with a more "modern" sound. However, Stoppard's diction remains resolutely British. His penchant for word play, and Stoppard's anti-romantic tendencies, push *Henry IV* uncomfortably far (to me) in the direction of comedy. This is as it should be; any good translator/adaptor reads the source play in light of their own experience and expectations, and presents, in the finished translation, an image of the original work. Stoppard's *Henry IV* is Tom Stoppard's imagination of what he thinks *Henry IV* to be.

For this version of *Henry IV* I wanted to recreate the play in modern, direct, and actable American English. I wanted to clarify the meaning and the point of the longer speeches, and capture as best I could both the dark comedy, and the deep vein of romantic melancholy that runs through the play. Language that's direct can still be poetic, and disappointed lovers are lovers still. What follows is my version of Pirandello's *Henry IV*; I hope you'll enjoy it. At the very least, I hope you'll find it a readable, clear and compelling introduction to this remarkable play.

Henry IV

(Enrico Quarto)

A TRAGEDY IN THREE ACTS

BY LUIGI PIRANDELLO

**Translated By
Royston Coppenger**

Characters.

"Henry IV"

The Marchioness Matilda Spina

Her Daughter Frida

The Young Marquis Charles Di Nolli

Baron Tito Belcredi

Doctor Dionysius Genoni

The Four Private Counsellors:
(The Names In Brackets Are Nicknames)

- o   Harold (Frank)
- o   Landolph (Lolo)
- o   Ordulph (Momo)
- o   Berthold (Fino)

John, an Elderly Waiter

Two Valets In Costume

An isolated villa in Italy; the time is the present.

ACT I

A salon in the villa, furnished and decorated so as to look exactly like the throne room of Henry IV in the royal residence at Goslar. Among the antique decorations there are two modern life-size portraits in oil. They are placed against the back wall, and mounted in a wooden stand that runs the whole length of the wall. (It is wide and protrudes, so that it is like a large bench). One of the paintings is on the right; the other on the left of the throne, which is in the middle of the wall and divides the stand.

The Imperial chair and Baldachin.

The two portraits represent a lady and a gentleman, both young, dressed up in carnival costumes: one as "Henry IV.," the other as the "Marchioness Matilda of Tuscany." Exits to Right and Left.

When the curtain goes up, the two valets jump down, as if surprised, from the stand on which they have been lying, and go and take their positions, as rigid as statues, on either side below the throne with their halberds in their hands. Soon after, from the second exit, right, enter Harold, Landolph, Ordulph and Berthold, young men employed by the Marquis Charles Di Nolli to play the part of "Secret Counsellors" at the court of "Henry IV." They are, therefore, dressed like German knights of the XIth century. Berthold, nicknamed Fino, is just entering on his duties for the first time. His companions are telling him what he has to do and amusing themselves at his expense. The scene is to be played rapidly and vivaciously.

LANDOLPH (*to Berthold as if explaining*). We call this "the throne room".

HAROLD. Goslar?

ORDULPH. Or at the Hartz castle, if you prefer.

HAROLD. Or at Wurms.

LANDOLPH. It could be anywhere, depending on his mood.

ORDULPH. Saxony.

HAROLD. Lombardy.

LANDOLPH. On the Rhine.

ONE OF THE VALETS (*Without moving, confused*). Excuse me . . .

HAROLD (*Turning around*). What?

FIRST VALET (*Standing stock-still*). Is he coming in? (*Alluding to Henry IV.*)

ORDULPH. No, no, he's sleeping. You can relax.

SECOND VALET (*Relaxes, taking a long breath and going to lie down again on the stand*). Why didn't you say so?

FIRST VALET (*Going over to Harold*). You got a light?

LANDOLPH. You aren't going to smoke a pipe, are you?

FIRST VALET (*While Harold offers him a light*). No; a cigarette. (*Lights his cigarette and lies down again on the stand*).

BERTHOLD (*Who has been looking on in amazement, walking round the room, regarding the costumes of the others*). I have to ask . . . this room . . . these clothes . . . I just don't understand. Which Henry IV is he? The French one? (*At this Landolph, Harold, and Ordulph, burst out laughing*).

LANDOLPH (*Still laughing; and pointing to Berth old as if inviting the others to make fun of him*). The French one! Don't be stupid!

ORDULPH. He thought he was the king of France!

HAROLD. Henry IV of Germany, of course: the Salian dynasty!

ORDULPH. The great and tragic Emperor!

LANDOLPH. The one who did penance in Canossa. Every day we fight the terrible battle between Church and State.

ORDULPH. The Empire against the Papacy!

HAROLD. Antipopes against the Pope!

LANDOLPH. Kings against antikings!

ORDULPH. War on the Saxons!

HAROLD. And don't forget the rebel Princes!

LANDOLPH. The Emperor's own sons!

BERTHOLD (*Covering his head with his hands to protect himself against this avalanche of information*). Okay, okay, I get it! I just had the wrong idea. So that's why these aren't sixteenth century costumes.

HAROLD. Sixteenth century? Not a chance.

ORDULPH. We're somewhere between a thousand and eleven hundred.

LANDOLPH. Work it out for yourself: he went to Canossa on the 25th of January, 1071 . . .

BERTHOLD (*More confused than ever*). Oh my God! I blew it!

ORDULPH. It's an honest mistake, thinking it was the French court.

BERTHOLD. But I've been studying the sixteenth century!

LANDOLPH. You're only about four hundred years off.

BERTHOLD (*Angrily*). Jesus! You should have told me it was Germany and not France. Do you have any idea how many books I've read in the past two weeks?

HAROLD. But didn't we tell you that poor Tito was Adelbert of Bremen?

BERTHOLD. No, I would have remembered that!

LANDOLPH. Well, look. When Tito died, the Marquis Di Nolli . . .

BERTHOLD. So it was him! He might have told me.

HAROLD. Maybe he thought you knew.

LANDOLPH. He didn't want to hire any more substitutes. He thought we'd be enough. But then he started pissing and moaning about "Adelbert being driven away" and all that, because of course he had no idea poor Tito was dead, so he thought the rival bishops of Cologne and Mayence had banished him . . .

BERTHOLD (*Rubbing his eyes wearily*). I haven't got the slightest idea what any of that means...

ORDULPH. That is a problem.

HAROLD. But what's worse is, even we don't know who you're supposed to be.

BERTHOLD. What? You're not serious!

ORDULPH. "Berthold." That's all we know.

BERTHOLD. But which Berthold? And why that name?

LANDOLPH (*Solemnly imitating Henry IV.*). "They've driven Adalbert away from me. I must see Berthold! I want Berthold !" That's all he said.

HAROLD. We had to look for a Berthold.

ORDULPH. And here you are.

LANDOLPH. Just try not to spoil things.

BERTHOLD (*Indignant, getting ready to go*). Okay, that's it. Forget it! Thanks, but no thanks.

HAROLD (*Restraining him with the other two, amid laughter*). Take it easy! Don't get excited!

LANDOLPH. Look on the bright side. None of us know who we really are. He's Harold, he's Ordulph, I'm Landolph. That's what he calls us. We're used to it. But we aren't real people, it's just old-fashioned names he picked out of the air. Same for you: Berthold? Just an old-sounding name he read somewhere. Poor Tito was the only one who had a deent part. The Bishop of Bremen was a real person, and Tito made the most of it. Poor bastard.

HAROLD. He studied so hard, poor guy!

LANDOLPH. Tito even ordered King Henry around, debated policy, gave him spiritual guidance. It was impressive. The three of us, on the other hand, are what's known as "secret counsellors" – because the history books all say that Henry IV was despised by the aristocracy for surrounding himself with young men from the bourgeoisie.

ORDULPH. Us, that is.

LANDOLPH. Just your average vassals, hard-drinking, hard-loving . . .

BERTHOLD. So I'm here to, what, entertain him?

HAROLD. To entertain his *fantasy*.

ORDULPH. It's not as easy as it sounds.

LANDOLPH We may *look* like we stepped out of a history book. And God knows, there's enough history for a thousand books in the reign of Henry IV. But the fact is, we don't do a damned thing. All show and no substance. The secret counselors of Henry IV? They must have been real characters, interesting, cunning, ruthless characters, improvising their way through court scandals, papal intrigues, always looking out for their own interests. As for us -? We just hang around, looking magnificent, waiting for him to move us around, put words in our mouths. We're not much more than glorified hand puppets.

HAROLD. Now, now, it's not that bad. There's a lot riding on our performances. If he asks a question and you don't give the right answer, there's hell to pay.

LANDOLPH. True enough.

BERTHOLD. Sweet Jesus, how am I supposed to give him the right answer? I studied Henry IV of France, and he turns out to be Henry IV of Germany! (*The other three laugh*).

HAROLD. You'd better hit the books again.

ORDULPH. We'll help you.

HAROLD. We're experts at this point. We'll start with a brief overview.

ORDULPH. Of course you know the basic story -?

HAROLD. Look! (*Turns him around and shows him the portrait of the Marchioness Matilda on the wall*). Who's that?

BERTHOLD (*Looking at it*). The woman? Um, she's certainly out of place. Both of them are. Two modern portraits here among all these relics, they must be important.

HAROLD. Very good! They weren't always here. The paintings are covering up two niches that were meant to hold statues.

LANDOLPH (*Interrupting and continuing*). Which would be a strange design choice if they really were paintings.

BERTHOLD. If they're not paintings, what are they?

LANDOLPH. Oh, they're paintings to the rest of us… Go on, touch them, see for yourself. But for *him*… (*Makes a mysterious gesture to the right, alluding to Henry IV*). . . he'll never touch them . . .

BERTHOLD. Why? What are they to him?

LANDOLPH. Nobody knows exactly, but I've got a pretty good idea. I think they're supposed to be mirrors. Reflecting back the world in his mind. You understand? That one is him, dressed in his costume, standing in this throne room. And the other one? It's his other mirror, reflecting his fantasy back into this world. When you've been here as long as we have, it'll make more sense.

BERTHOLD. So I'll go crazy too, is that what you're saying?

HAROLD. Don't say that word! Crazy. Look at it as an adventure.

BERTHOLD. How did you all learn your parts?

LANDOLPH. You can't live 800 years in the past without picking up a few things.

HAROLD. Don't worry. You'll get into the spirit of things in no time.

ORDULPH. It might even make you a better person.

BERTHOLD. Well, for Christ's sake, help me out! Give me a few main lines, anyway.

HAROLD. Let us do the talking. Follow our lead.

LANDOLPH. You'll be a first-class puppet in no time. (*They take him by the arm to lead him away*).

BERTHOLD (*Stopping and looking at the portrait on the wall*). Wait a minute! You haven't told me who the lady is. Is she the Emperor's wife?

HAROLD. No! The Emperor's wife is Bertha of Susa, the sister of Amadeus II of Savoy.

ORDULPH. And the Emperor, who prefers more lively company, can't stand her, and wants to put her away.

LANDOLPH. This woman is his most ferocious enemy: Matilda, Marchioness of Tuscany.

BERTHOLD. Oh, wait! I've heard of her! She let the Pope stay at her house...?

LANDOLPH. Exactly: at Canossa!

ORDULPH. Pope Gregory VII!

HAROLD. Our chief antagonist. Come on! Let's go! (*All four move toward the right to go out, when, from the left, the old servant John enters in evening dress*).

JOHN (*Quickly, anxiously*). Hey! Hey, Frank! Lolo!

HAROLD (*Spinning around*). What?

BERTHOLD (*Astonished to see a man in modern clothes enter the throne room*). Whoa, whoa, wait a second!

LANDOLPH. A 20th- century man, here! Get out! Go! (*They run over to him, pretending to menace him and throw him out*).

ORDULPH (*Heroically*). Lackey of Gregory VII., away!

HAROLD. Away! Away!

JOHN (*Annoyed, defending himself*). Oh, stop it! Stop it!

ORDULPH. No, you can't come in here!

HAROLD. Away with him!

LANDOLPH (*To Berthold*). It's black magic, boy! A foul fiend conjured by the Wizard of Rome! Out with your swords! (*Makes as if to draw a sword*).

JOHN (*Shouting*). Stop playing around! The Marquis is here! And he brought friends . . .

LANDOLPH. The more the merrier! Any women?

ORDULPH. Old or young?

JOHN. There are two gentlemen.

HAROLD. Oh, who cares? What about the women?

JOHN. The Marchioness and her daughter.

LANDOLPH (*Surprised*). What?

ORDULPH. The Marchioness?

JOHN. Yes! The Marchioness!

HAROLD. Who are the others?

JOHN. I don't know.

HAROLD (*To Berthold*). They're coming to bring us a message from the Pope, do you see?

ORDULPH. All messengers of Gregory VII! What fun!

JOHN. Will you please let me talk?

HAROLD. By all means.

JOHN. I think one of the men is a doctor.

LANDOLPH. Nothing new about that.

HAROLD. Berthold, I think you're good luck!

LANDOLPH. Watch how we handle this doctor!

BERTHOLD. Should I be worried?

JOHN. If you would *please* let me finish . . . they want to come into the throne room.

LANDOLPH (*Shocked*). What? Her too? The Marchioness wants to come in here?

HAROLD. That changes everything. This is no joke.

LANDOLPH. We'll be cast in a real tragedy this time.

BERTHOLD (*Curious*). Why? Why?

ORDULPH (*Pointing to the portrait*). That's a picture of her, don't you understand?

LANDOLPH. The daughter is engaged to the Marquis. But why would they come here?

ORDULPH. If he sees her, he'll go wild.

LANDOLPH. Maybe he won't recognize her any more.

JOHN. Make sure he stays in his room.

ORDULPH. Easier said than done.

HAROLD. You know what he's like!

JOHN. Tie him to the bed if you have to! That's an order! Now go!

HAROLD. What if he's already awake?

ORDULPH. Let's hurry!

LANDOLPH (*Going towards John with the others*). I want a full explanation. Later.

JOHN (*Shouting after them*). Close the door, and hide the key! That other door too. (*Pointing to the other door on right*).

JOHN (*To the two valets*). Well, you too! There (*Pointing to exit right*)! Close the door after you, and hide the key!

(The two valets go out by the first door on right. John moves over to the left to show in: Donna Matilda Spina, the young Marchioness Frida, Dr. Dionysius Genoni, the Baron Tito Belcredi and the young Marquis Charles Di Nolli, who, as master of the house, enters last.)

DONNA MATILDA SPINA is about 45. She's still attractive, but she's started trying to cover the ravages of time with make-up. Her face has the motionless appearance of a wax statue. This facial make-up contrasts with her beautiful sad mouth. A widow for many years, she now has as her friend the Baron Tito Belcredi. To all appearances, she doesn't take Belcredi very seriously. Nor does anybody else.

What TITO BELCREDI really does for her, he alone knows; this gives him the freedom to laugh at her pretense that she doesn't need him. He can even laugh at the jokes she makes at his expense. He is younger than the Marchioness, slim, prematurely gray. His head is bird-like in shape. He could be a very animated person – unknown to most of his acquaintances, he's a formidable swordsman - but he hides athletic gifts beneath a mask of spoiled indolence. He speaks in an affected, nasal, laconic drawl.

FRIDA, the daughter of the Marchioness is 19. She's obsessed with her own sorrows, most of which boil down to the fact that she's no match for her beautiful, accomplished mother. Frida feels personally tainted by all the gossip her mother attracts. Fortunately for her, she's engaged to the Marquis Charles Di Nolli.

CHARLES DI NOLLI is a very proper and reserved young man. He's unfailingly kind toward others, but at the same time he has a high estimate of his own importance. He broods obsessively about all the responsibilities he imagines others place upon him. He is dressed in mourning for the recent death of his mother.

Dr. DIONYSIUS GENONI has a bold, ruddy, sensual face, bulging eyes, and a silvery beard waxed into a precise point. His manners are elegant and practiced. He is all but bald.

All enter hesitantly, like children walking into a haunted house. All of them (except Di Nolli) stare wide-eyed around the room. At first, they speak in choked whispers.

DI NOLLI (*To John*). You told them?

JOHN. Yes, my Lord; it's all taken care of.

BELCREDI. It's perfect! Perfect!

DOCTOR. Fascinating! His mania has projected itself into every inch of this room.

DONNA MATILDA (*Glancing round for her portrait, discovers it, and goes up close to it*). See? What did I tell you. (*Going back to admire it, while mixed emotions stir within her*). Yes . . . yes . . . (*Calls her daughter Frida*).

FRIDA. Oh, your portrait.

DONNA MATILDA. No, no . . . look again: it's your face, not mine. Not any more.

DI NOLLI. That's just what I was saying . . .

DONNA MATILDA. I would never have thought... (*Shaking as if with a chill*) It gives me a strange feeling. (*Then looking at her daughter*). Frida, what's wrong? (*She pulls her to her side, and slips an arm round her waist*). Come: don't you see yourself in me there?

FRIDA. Well, I really . . .

DONNA MATILDA. Don't you think so? Be honest! (*Turning to Belcredi*) Look at it, Tito! What do you think?

BELCREDI (*without looking*). No, no! I'm not getting involved. Absolutely not!

DONNA MATILDA. Idiot! You think I'm fishing for compliments? (*Turing to Doctor Genoni*). What do you say, Doctor? Say something, please!

The Doctor makes a move to go near to the picture.

BELCREDI (*With his back turned, pretending to attract his attention secretly*) . . . Hss! Doctor! For the God's sake, leave it alone!

DOCTOR (*Bewildered, smiling*). I don't understand.

DONNA MATILDA. Don't listen to him! Come here! He's unbearable!

FRIDA. It's his job to act the fool, don't you know that by now?

BELCREDI (*To the Doctor, seeing him go over*). Watch your foot, doctor! Mind where you're going!

DOCTOR. What?

BELCREDI. Be careful it doesn't fly into your mouth!

DOCTOR (*Laughing feebly*). Ha, very good. But there's nothing controversial about saying that a daughter resembles her mother.

BELCREDI. Oh, my God. Now he's done it.

DONNA MATILDA (*With exaggerated anger, advancing towards Belcredi*). What's the matter? What did he say?

DOCTOR (*Candidly*). Just a simple statement of fact.

BELCREDI (*Answering the Marchioness*). He said there was nothing surprising about it -- and you're surprised! Why should that be, if you're trying to grow old with dignity?

DONNA MATILDA (*Still more angry*). You idiot! Yes, it's natural, that's the point! That isn't my daughter's portrait. (*Pointing to the canvas*). It's mine. I'm surprised to see it looks so much like my daughter. That's it. I was being perfectly sincere. Stop with your jokes.

FRIDA (*Slowly and wearily*). My God! It's always like this . . . fighting about nothing. . .

BELCREDI (*Slowly, looking dejected, apologetically*). I wasn't joking. I noticed that Frida didn't share your opinion, that's all.

DONNA MATILDA. Naturally! I see myself in her at that age so clearly, and she can't stand the comparison.

DOCTOR. That's understandable. For the young lady your portrait is a relic, it's ancient history, while, for the Marchioness, it brings everything back: movements, gestures, looks, smiles, a whole life of memories...

DONNA MATILDA. Exactly!

DOCTOR (*Continuing, turning towards her*). Naturally enough, you can relive all those old sensations through your daughter.

DONNA MATILDA. Forget it, the moment has passed. Why do you have to ruin everything?

DOCTOR (*Startled, adopting a professorial tone*). It's difficult to say where likeness comes from. A full explanation would require...

BELCREDI (*Interrupting*) Careful! Attracting her ladyship's scorn... that's *my* job!

DI NOLLI. Oh, Give it a rest, will you? (*Points to the two doors on the Right, as a warning that there is someone there who may be listening*). We've got not time to waste.

FRIDA. Tell him. (*Alluding to Belcredi*).

DI NOLLI. That's enough! We're here with the Doctor; and we're here for a very important reason. To me, at least.

DOCTOR. Yes, yes, of course. First of all, the facts in the case. Marchioness... with your permission... can you tell me why your portrait is here? Did you give it to him?

DONNA MATILDA. No, no, of course not. Why would I? I was Frida's age when this was painted – it wouldn't have been proper. I sent him the painting three or four years after his accident. It was your mother's idea. (*Points at Di Nolli*) . . .

DOCTOR. She's his sister? (*Alluding to Henry IV.*)

DI NOLLI. Was, doctor. She died a month ago. It was her wish that we come here. Otherwise Frida and I would be taking a very different trip together right now...

DOCTOR ... for a very different cure!

DI NOLLI. Please. My mother died believing her dear little brother could be cured.

DOCTOR. What made her think so?

DI NOLLI. He said some... strange things shortly before Mother died.

DOCTOR. Really! What kind of things?

DI NOLLI. No idea. I only know that my mother was terribly upset by her last visit with him. On her death-bed, she made me promise that I would never neglect him, that I would have doctors see him, and examine him.

DOCTOR. So it was something small.... Small but significant! And this portrait?

DONNA MATILDA. The portrait is neither here nor there. It just startled me because I hadn't seen the thing in so long.

DOCTOR. Yes, yes, but hold on . . .

DI NOLLI. What's it been, fifteen years?

DONNA MATILDA. More like eighteen!

DOCTOR. You're not listening. I think these two portraits are of the utmost significance. They were painted before that pageant, weren't they? Before all the bad things that followed?

DONNA MATILDA. Of course!

DOCTOR. So when these were painted... he was still in his right mind. Did he suggest you have your portrait painted?

DONNA MATILDA. Lots of people who took part in the pageant had their portraits done as souvenirs...

BELCREDI. I had mine done -- as "Charles of Anjou !"

DONNA MATILDA... as soon as the costumes were ready.

BELCREDI. In fact, some people thought all our portraits should stay together on pemanent display in the ballroom where the pageant took place. But everybody wanted to hang on to their little souvenirs.

DONNA MATILDA. I didn't mind letting it go. Especially for your mother... (*Indicates Di Nolli*).

DOCTOR. But did he ask for it himself?

DONNA MATILDA. Ah, that I don't remember . . . Maybe it was only his sister, wanting to help out . . .

DOCTOR. One other thing: this pageant, was it his idea?

BELCREDI (*At once*). No, no, it was mine!

DOCTOR. If you please . . .

DONNA MATILDA. Don't listen to him! It was poor Belassi's idea.

BELCREDI. Belassi! He had *nothing* to do with it!

DONNA MATILDA. Count Belassi died, poor thing, two or three months later . . .

BELCREDI. Belassi wasn't anywhere around . . .

DI NOLLI. Doctor, what difference does it make who had the original idea?

DOCTOR. It might help me make a determination...

BELCREDI. It was my idea! Not that I'm proud of it, given what happened. It was like this: one night, early November it was, I was reading an illustrated German magazine at my club. I mean, I was looking at the pictures, I can't read German, thank you very much. There was this picture of the Kaiser, visiting the town where he'd gone to college. I can't remember which town it was....

DOCTOR. It was Bonn, of course!

BELCREDI. All right, Bonn. Whatever. The Kaiser was riding a horse, dressed up in one of those old-fashioned student guild costumes, followed by a whole procession of students dressed up the same way. That picture stuck with me. And then somebody at the club said we should stage a pageant for the upcoming carnival, and I said, "Why don't we each pick famous people from history – kings, queens, emperors, popes – and all make our entrance on horseback?" Everybody thought it was a great idea...

DONNA MATILDA. Belassi's the one who invited me.

BELCREDI. Well, Belassi was a bald-faced liar! God rest his soul. If Belassi told you it was his idea, he was lying. Belassi wasn't even at the club the night I had the idea. Neither was he (*Meaning Henry IV.*)

DOCTOR. Why did he choose the character of Henry IV?

DONNA MATILDA. It was my doing. I said I'd be the Marchioness Matilda of Tuscany. Just because of my name. It was just an idea.

DOCTOR. I . . . What does that have to do with Henry IV?

DONNA MATILDA. I had no idea myself at first. He said he'd be at my feet like Henry IV at Canossa. I'd heard of Canossa, of course, but I didn't remember much about the story. And then I learned that Matilda was close friends with Pope Gregory VII, the deadly enemy of Henry IV. And so without meaning to, I fell into that whole sorry history, which is why he decided to ride beside me in the pageant as Henry IV.

DOCTOR. Because . . .

23

BELCREDI. For Christ's sake, Doctor, because he was head over heels in love with her! (*Indicates the Marchioness*)! And naturally . . .

DONNA MATILDA. Naturally? There was nothing natural about it . . .

BELCREDI (*Pointing to her*). She couldn't stand him . . .

DONNA MATILDA. That's not true! I didn't dislike him. Not at all! But for me, at that time, when a man started to get too serious....

BELCREDI (*Continuing for her*). You naturally assumed he was an idiot.

DONNA MATILDA. Not in this case; not like with you.

BELCREDI. I never asked you to take me seriously.

DONNA MATILDA. Don't remind me. But with him there was no joking. (*To the Doctor, her tone changing*) One of the greatest trials we women have to face, Doctor, is seeing that look of eternal devotion in a man's eyes. (*Bursts out laughing*) There's nothing quite so ridiculous. If men could only see themselves the way we see them! I've never been able to see that look in a man's eyes without laughing. But twenty years ago – how can I say this? – I confess that when I laughed at him, it was partly out of fear. His eyes were so deep, so sad, I almost wanted to believe him. But I saw something dangerous in him, even then.

DOCTOR (*With keen interest*). Very interesting! Dangerous, you say?

DONNA MATILDA. Yes, dangerous. He was different from the others. And me, I'm... well... I don't have any patience for men who are too serious. And I was so young. And a woman. I didn't think I was brave enough to deal with true devotion. So I laughed at him. A lot of people laughed at him, all those silly, shallow people made fun of him behind his back, and I joined in. But I hated myself for it.

BELCREDI. I know how he must have felt!

DONNA MATILDA. You invite laughter, my dear, it's your only social grace. It was different with him. Completely different. You <u>let</u> people laugh in your face.

BELCREDI. Better in my face than behind my back!

DOCTOR. Let's stick to the subject. I understand he was already considered eccentric in those days.

BELCREDI. You could say that.

DOCTOR. In what way?

BELCREDI. He was a bit… obsessive.

DONNA MATILDA. Not at all! I'll tell you how it was. Yes, he stood out in our little society; but only because he loved things so much.

BELCREDI. I didn't say he was faking it. Not at all, I think he was sincerely caught up in all his passions. But it was something of a pose at the same time. He was… watching himself go overboard. And I think it made him suffer at times. He would fly into fits of rage at himself. It was almost comical.

DOCTOR. Really?

DONNA MATILDA. I suppose.

BELCREDI (*To Donna Matilda*). And you know why? (*To the doctor*). This is my theory. When you act a part, it can feel very exciting. But it puts you out of touch with yourself. You become a lie. But it's a lie you've committed to. He could be very sincere, but then he would have these fits of exaggeration, affectation, call it what you will. As if he was trying to distract himself, forget himself. He was fascinating until you really got to know him. Then all his flights of fancy seemed shallow, childish, and… sometimes… ridiculous.

DOCTOR. So he was antisocial?

BELCREDI. Not at all. His parties were legendary, he was constantly throwing events for charity – dances, stage plays, tableaux vivants, things like that. He could be a lot of fun. He loved to perform whenever he could. He was a talented actor, you know.

DI NOLLI. He's brilliant, now that he's lost his mind.

25

BELCREDI. He was even then. And then the accident happened, when the horse fell . . .

DOCTOR. Hit the back of his head, didn't he?

DONNA MATILDA. It was horrible! I was right there when it happened! I saw him on the ground, the horse trampling him...

BELCREDI. Nobody realized how serious it was. The pageant stopped for a moment, things were a little chaotic. People wondered what was going on. But they'd already taken him away, and the pageant went on as if nothing happened.

DONNA MATILDA. There was no wound. No blood.

BELCREDI. We thought he'd just fainted.

DONNA MATILDA. But two hours later . . .

BELCREDI. He came into the drawing-room of the villa . . .

DONNA MATILDA. My God! You could see it in his face.

BELCREDI. That's not true. Nobody could tell at first.

DONNA MATILDA. None of you were paying attention.

BELCREDI. Everybody was still in character. We thought it was a joke.

DONNA MATILDA. And then, doctor... imagine how horrible it was, as we began to realize that *he wasn't acting*.

DOCTOR. So it happened there, with everyone around?

BELCREDI. Yes! He took over the room. We thought he'd recovered, that he was pretending – like all of us, except doing it considerably better. He was known to be a good actor.

DONNA MATILDA. Some of the guests started to hit him with their whips and fans and sticks. All in fun, of course.

BELCREDI. And then -- he drew his sword and lunged at us . . . It was terrifying.

DONNA MATILDA. I'll never forget it. A circle of masked faces, staring in terror at him. And his face, with the mask of madness over it. Horrible.

BELCREDI. He was Henry IV, Henry IV in person, burning with rage.

DONNA MATILDA. He'd spent a month studying Henry IV to get ready for the pageant – you see how obsessive he could be? – and now it all came pouring out of him. It was terrifying.

DOCTOR. Yes, well, it makes some sense. A dilettante's passing fancy becomes fixed, hardened, due to the damage to his brain.

BELCREDI (*To Frida and Di Nolli*). Life can play some cruel jokes, can't it? (*To Di Nolli*): You were four or five years old. (*To Frida*) Your mother sees you in her old portrait; but when it was painted she didn't have the slightest idea you would ever exist. My hair's already going grey; and as for him -- (*Points to portrait*) -- ha! He fell off a horse, and never got up. Henry IV forever!

DOCTOR (*Drawing himself up importantly*). Well, well, now, we've got all our facts on the table...

(*Suddenly Berhtold rushes in through the first entrance on the right, closest to the audience. He is in a state of great agitation*)

BERTHOLD (*Rushing in*). Oh, thank God! (*Everyone recoils in terror; Berthold stops in his tracks, confused*).

FRIDA (*Running away terrified*). It's him! He's broken loose! . . .

DONNA MATILDA (*Covering her face with her hands so as not to see*). I can't stand to watch this!

DI NOLLI. Calm down, calm down, it's not him!

DOCTOR. Who is it then?

BELCREDI. Somebody we hired.

DI NOLLI. We pay four young men to keep an eye on him; this is one of them.

BERTHOLD. Marquis, I'm very sorry . . .

DI NOLLI. It's too late for apologies! I told you to keep the doors shut and not disturb us.

BERTHOLD. I know that, but I can't take any more. Please, I want out of this job.

DI NOLLI. Wait, are you the new man? You just started a few hours ago.

BERTHOLD. Yes, sir, and I can't stand it, I can't.

DONNA MATILDA (*To Di Nolli excitedly*). Why? Has he gotten violent?

BERTHOLD (*quickly*). No, no, your ladyship – it's not him. It's the rest of the staff. You say "help manage his delusions", but they're only making things worse. I think they're the crazy ones. This is my first day on the job, and instead of helping me...

(*Landolph and Harold come in from the same door, but hesitate on the threshold*).

LANDOLPH. Excuse me?

HAROLD. May we come in?

DI NOLLI. Yes, yes, come. What's going on? What's the problem?

FRIDA. Oh God! I'm so anxious! I've got to get out of here. (*Makes towards exit at Left*).

DI NOLLI (*Restraining her at once*). You can't leave, Frida!

LANDOLPH. My Lord, this numbskull. . . (*indicates Berthold*).

BERTHOLD (*Protesting*). I'm not doing this! There's nothing to discuss! Goodbye!

LANDOLPH. You mean you're leaving?

HAROLD. He's going to ruin everything!

LANDOLPH. This fool managed to offend Henry IV in his first audience. We've been ordered to arrest him; we're supposed to drag in him front of the throne for summary judgment. What are we supposed to do now?

DI NOLLI. Shut the door. Shut the door! Now! (*Landolph goes over to close it*).

HAROLD. Ordulph can't handle him all by himself.

LANDOLPH. My Lord, I think we should change our plans. Announce the visitors right away. Maybe it'll distract him. Do you all have your stories straight?

DI NOLLI. It's all been arranged! (*To the Doctor*) Doctor, are you ready?

FRIDA. I'm not going! I'm not going! Leave me out of this. You too, mother, for God's sake, let's get out of here!

DOCTOR. But. . . he's not armed, is he?

DI NOLLI. Of course not. (*To Frida*): Frida, stop acting like a child. You insisted on coming.

FRIDA. No I didn't. It was mother's idea.

DONNA MATILDA. And I'm ready to get started. What do we do?

BELCREDI. Are the costumes absolutely necessary?

LANDOLPH. Absolutely, sir. Unfortunately. (*Showing his costume*) If you walked in there in modern clothes, no telling what might happen...

HAROLD. He'd think you were... demons, or travelling minstrels, or something.

DI NOLLI. In his eyes our modern fashions would look like outlandish costumes. Scandalous.

LANDOLPH. And the worst part is, he'd assume you were sent by his mortal enemy.

BELCREDI. Pope Gregory VII?

LANDOLPH. Exactly. He calls him "a pagan."

BELCREDI. He calls the Pope a pagan? That's good.

LANDOLPH. A pagan and a necromancer. And the most powerful dark wizard in Europe. He's terribly afraid of the Pope.

DOCTOR. Persecution mania!

HAROLD. It would send him right over the edge.

DI NOLLI (*To Belcredi*). You don't have to see him, you know. The Doctor could go without us.

DOCTOR. – Wh...wh...what? By myself?

DI NOLLI. They'd be with you. (*Indicates the three young men*).

DOCTOR. It's not that I'm afraid . . . But I thought the Marchioness . . .

DONNA MATILDA. Of course. I'm going to see him. I want to.

FRIDA. Why, mother, why? Please, let's just go!

DONNA MATILDA (*Imperiously*). Don't make this any harder than it already is! He's the reason I came here today. (*To Landolph*) Introduce me as "Adelaide," the mother.

LANDOLPH. Right! The mother of the Empress Bertha. Good! You can wear a crown, and I think we've got a robe that'll hide your clothes completely. (*To Harold*): Harold, go get her costume.

HAROLD. Wait a minute! What about him? (*Pointing at the Doctor*)

DOCTOR. Oh yes . . . we decided ... that is to say, the suggestion was . . . the Bishop of Cluny, Hugh of Cluny!

HAROLD. Abbot, not Bishop. All right. Hugh of Cluny.

LANDOLPH. He's been a frequent guest under this roof.

DOCTOR (*amazed*). What? He's been here before?

LANDOLPH. It's all right! I just mean it's an easy disguise to take on.

HAROLD. We've used it before, with other guests.

DOCTOR. But . . .

LANDOLPH. He doesn't care what Hugh of Cluny looks like. As long as you're wearing the right clothes.

DONNA MATILDA. I hope that's true of me as well.

DI NOLLI. All right, Frida, I'll take you home. Come on, Tito!

BELCREDI. No. No. If she's staying, so am I.

DONNA MATILDA. I don't need your help.

BELCREDI. Maybe you don't. But I'd like to see him again. All right?

LANDOLPH. Well, to be honest, three might be better.

HAROLD. But what will he wear?

BELCREDI. Make it something easy, will you?

LANDOLPH (*to Harold*). Hmm. Okay, let him be some guy from Cluny.

BELCREDI. What do you mean "some guy from Cluny"?

LANDOLPH. A Benedictine monk from the Abbey of Cluny. You can be in attendance on the Abbot. (*To Harold*): Get a move on! (*To Berthold*). You help Harold fetch the costumes. And then go hide somewhere. Don't show your face for the rest of the day. (*To Harold*): As soon as they're squared away, go announce the visit of "Duchess Adelaide" and "Monsignor Hugh of Cluny." Got it? (*Harold and Berthold go off by the first door on the Right*).

DI NOLLI. We'll leave now. (*Goes off with Frida, left*).

DOCTOR. Does he… does he like Hugh of Cluny?

LANDOLPH. Oh, very much! Don't worry about that! The Abbot has always been treated with great respect here. He'll be happy to see you too, my Lady. You two are the reason he was able to get into the Castle of Canossa and meet Gregory VII in the first place. He never forgets a favor.

BELCREDI. And what do I do?

LANDOLPH. Keep a respectful distance and don't say much.

DONNA MATILDA (*Irritated, nervous*). It would really be better if you went home.

BELCREDI (*Slowly, spitefully*). You're awfully worried about this meeting.

DONNA MATILDA (*Haughtily*). So what? That's none of your business.

(*Berthold comes in with the costumes*).

LANDOLPH (*Seeing him enter*). Here are the costumes. This robe is for the Marchioness . . .

DONNA MATILDA. Wait a minute! Let me take my hat off. (*Does so and gives it to Berthold*).

LANDOLPH. Just lay it aside. (*Then to the Marchioness, while he offers to put the ducal crown on her head*). Allow me!

DONNA MATILDA. Is there a mirror in this room?

LANDOLPH. Yes, in there (*Points to the door on the Left*). If you'd rather dress yourself...

DONNA MATILDA. I think that would be advisable. (*Takes up her hat and goes off with Berthold, who carries the cloak and the crown*).

BELCREDI. (*Looking at his robes*) Well, I ended up in the priesthood after all. Isn't it expensive, keeping all these costumes around?

THE DOCTOR. Illusions cost money.

BELCREDI. Then it's lucky for him he's rich.

LANDOLPH. I've commissioned a whole roomful of period costumes. They're made by some of the best theatrical costume designers. It isn't cheap.

(*Donna Matilda re-enters, wearing robe and crown*)

BELCREDI (*At once, in admiration*). You look wonderful!

DONNA MATILDA (*Looking at Belcredi and bursting into laughter*). And you look ridiculous. This will never work. You look like an ostrich wearing a dress.

BELCREDI. Well, what about the doctor?

THE DOCTOR. I don't think I look so bad, do I?

DONNA MATILDA. The doctor looks fine. But you! I don't know if I can keep a straight face.

THE DOCTOR. Does he see people often?

LANDOLPH. It depends. Sometimes he'll issue decrees, "such-and-such-a person is summoned into the royal" etcetera. Then we have to go out and find somebody who's willing to play the part. Women too...

DONNA MATILDA (*Hurt, but trying to hide the fact*). Women?

LANDOLPH. Um, yes. Quite a few in the first years.

BELCREDI (*Laughing*). That must have been amazing! In costume, like the Marchioness?

LANDOLPH. For women who... do that sort of work.... I don't think a little play acting is such a stretch.

BELCREDI. I suppose you're right. (*Ominously, to the Marchioness*) Be careful. I sense some danger for you in all this.

(*The second door on the right opens, and Harold appears; he quietly signals that everyone should stop talking*).

HAROLD. His Majesty, the Emperor!

(*The two valets enter first, and go and stand on either side of the throne. Then Henry IV comes in between Ordulph and Harold, who keep a little in the rear respectfully.*

HENRY IV is about 50 and very pale. The hair on the back of his head is already grey; over the temples and forehead it appears blond, owing to an amateurish dye job. On his cheek bones he has two small, doll-like dabs of blush, that stand out prominently against the rest of his deathly pallor. He is wearing a penitent's sack over his royal robes, as the real Henry IV did at Canossa. His eyes have a direct and commanding stare; this expression stands in strained contrast with the sackcloth. Ordulph carries the Imperial crown; Harold, the sceptre with the eagle, and the globe with the cross).

HENRY IV. (*Bowing first to Donna Matilda and afterwards to the doctor*). My lady . . . Monsignor . . . (*Then he looks at Belcredi and seems about to greet him too; when, suddenly, he turns to Landolph, and asks quietly*) Is that Peter Damiani?

LANDOLPH. No, Sire. He's just another monk from Cluny. He serves the Abbot.

(*Henry IV looks at Belcredi with increasing mistrust. Belcredi glances uncomfortably at the Doctor and the Marchioness. Suddenly Henry IV leaps up from the throne and cries out*)

HENRY IV. No, it's Peter Damiani! Don't try to hide it, father. (*Then turning quickly to Donna Matilda and the doctor as though to ward off a danger*) I swear! I swear on my life that my heart is changed toward your daughter. I admit I was going to divorce her; but he (*Indicating Belcredi*) forbade me in the name of Pope Alexander. Yes, yes, there were people ready to approve my divorce: the Bishop of Mayence would have done it in exchange for a few thousand acres. (*Looks at Landolph a little perplexed and adds*): But ... uh, I'm not criticizing the bishops. (*More humbly to Belcredi*) I'm grateful to you, believe me, I'm grateful to you for stopping me ! God knows, my life is nothing but a series of humiliations: my mother, Adalbert, Tribur, Goslar! And now this! Sackcloth and ashes. (*Changing tone suddenly: to himself, like an actor running through his lines*). Enough of this. Be clear, be firm, be patient. No matter what. (*Then turning to all and speaking solemnly*). I know how to make amends for the mistakes of my past; and I can humble myself even before you, Peter Damiani. (*Bows deeply to him and keeps his head bowed. Then, with growing suspicion*). Were you the one who started that obscene rumor about my mother and the Bishop of Augusta?

BELCREDI (*Since Henry IV has his finger pointed at him*). Me? No, I never . . .

HENRY IV. (*Straightening up*). Are you calling me a liar, you rogue? (*Staring at Belcredi*) I would never have believed it. (*Goes to the doctor and plucks his sleeve, while winking at him knowingly*) Some things never change, Monsignor. Bishops!

HAROLD (*Softly, whispering as if to prompt the doctor*). Yes, yes, the rapacious bishops!

THE DOCTOR (*To Harold, trying to follow him*). Yes, yes, those disgrace . . . um. . .

HENRY IV. Nothing satisfies them! I was a little boy, Monsignor . . . Playing happily in my garden, completely unaware of the awful responsibility that had descended upon me. I was six years old; and they tore me away from my mother, and made use of me against her without my knowledge . . . and stealing, stealing! . . . Each one was worse than the other . . . Hanno worse than Stephen! Stephen worse than Hanno!

LANDOLPH (*Softly, persuasively, to call his attention*). Your Majesty?

HENRY IV. (*Turning round quickly*). Quite right . . . this is no time to talk against the bishops. But those rumors about my mother, Monsignor – that I won't stand for. (*Looks at the Marchioness and grows tender*). I can't even shed tears for her, Lady . . . You have a mother's heart, you'll understand this. They told me she died when I was a child. And then, a month ago, she came to visit me from the convent where she'd been living in hiding. (*Sustained pause full of feeling. Then smiling sadly*) But I can't cry about my mother; because if you're here now, and I'm dressed like this (*shows the sackcloth he is wearing*), it means I'm only twenty-six years old, I haven't learned the truth about her yet.

HAROLD. And so she's still alive, Majesty! . . .

ORDULPH. Just hidden away in her convent!

HENRY IV. (*Looking at them*). That's right! So I'll save my grief for another time. (*Shows the Marchioness his dyed hair, somewhat flirtatiously*). Look! I'm still boyish . . . (*Then slowly as if in confidence*). Enough of these games. In the present company there's no need. But attention to detail... We bide our time, Monsignor, do you understand? (*Turns to the Marchioness and notices her hair, admiringly*). Nicely done... Do you color it yourself? God knows I'm not judging! Nobody likes to grow old. We're born, we die, but in between... Did you ask to be born, Monsignor? I didn't! That's how life is. One thing after another we never asked for, never wanted. We do the best we can.

DOCTOR. (*Stalling for time while he studies Henry IV*) Very true...
um, forsooth.

HENRY IV. I'll tell you something I've learned: When people aren't
resigned to their fates, desire spins out of control. A woman wants to be
a man... an old man longs to have his youth back. It's obviously
ridiculous. Unchecked desire makes people want what they can never
have. But listen, Monsignor. Even those desires we can fulfill – the
reasonable ones, the ones life is willing to grant – those are equally
ridiculous. We each have an identity we cling to. But while we hold
ourselves in check, trying not to violate our deeply held sense of self –
suddenly something rears its head, like a serpent in the garden. Life
takes over. (*To the Marchioness*) Have you never been surprised by
what you're capable of? Have you always been exactly who you want
to be? My God. Don't you ever ask yourself: on such-and-such a day,
how was I able to do the thing I did? (*Fixing her intently with his gaze*)
You know what I mean. But don't worry. Your secret's safe with me.
And you, Peter Damiani, how did you come to befriend that man?

LANDOLPH. Your highness...?

HENRY IV. (*Suddenly*). I won't say his name! (*Turning to Belcredi*):
What did he seem like to you? We all have an image of ourselves we
cling to desperately. So what? My dyed hair looks ridiculous to you,
but if it makes me happy what's the harm? Our Lady here doesn't dye
her hair to fool other people, or even to fool herself – but just to
deceive her own image in the mirror for a few more years. We're all in
costume all the time; maybe it's a joke to me, maybe it's serious for
her. I'm not talking about the crown, the robes she wears – I'm talking
about the image of her lost youth she wants to preserve like a fly in
amber. And as for you, Damiani – the memory of your past lives inside
you like a dream, like a catalog of possible lives. I'm in the same boat.
I have so many strange memories – like dreams I can only half
remember. And tomorrow this day will be nothing but another dream.
(*Suddenly he pulls violently at his sackcloth*) This sackcloth ... (*Trying
furiously to pull it off, as his three valets run over and try to prevent
him*) Ah, God! (*Ripping of the sackcloth*) Tomorrow, at Bressanone, the
German and Lombard bishops will come over to my side. We'll sign
the act deposing Pope Gregory VII. And then he won't be Pope at all!
Just a poor, homeless monk!

ORDULPH (*With the other three*). Your highness! For God's sake! . . .

HAROLD *(Trying to put the sackcloth over Henry IV's head again)*. Listen to him, your highness!

LANDOLPH. The Monsignor came here with the Duchess to intercede on your behalf. (*Makes secret signs to the Doctor to say something at once*).

DOCTOR (*Confused*). Ah yes . . . yes . . . absolutely . . .

HENRY IV. (*Repeating at once, almost terrified, allowing the three to put on the sackcloth again, and pulling it down over him with his own hands*). Intercede . . . yes . . . yes . . . forgive me, Monsignor: forgive me, my Lady . . . It's a terrible burden, being excommunicated. (*Bends over, clutching his face with his hands, as though waiting for something to crush him. Then changing tone, but without moving, says softly to Landolph, Harold and Ordulph*): But for some reason, I just can't humble myself with that man standing there! (*Indicates Belcredi*).

LANDOLPH (*Softly*). That's because you think he's Peter Damiani, your highness. But he's someone else altogether.

HENRY IV. (*Peeking at Belcredi through his fingers*). He's not Peter Damiani?

HAROLD. No, no, he's a common monk, highness.

HENRY IV. (*Sadly, but with a tinge of agitation*) Sometimes I can't control my thoughts... You – you understand me, don't you? Women understand things, and as a Duchess – This moment could decide everything. I could join forces with the Lombard bishops, overthrow the Pope, lock him in the dungeon, and run off to Rome to elect an anti-pope. Robert Guiscard would smile on me then, and Gregory VII would be finished. It's tempting. But I'm smart enough to resist. A good Pope is a rare man in these times – someone who does his job and knows his place. You think it's some kind of joke, this sackcloth I'm wearing. But you're wrong. I'm a gambler. I'm betting that when the dust settles, Gregory VII will still be on top. Maybe tomorrow I'll rewrite this little play, and you'll get to see the pope in chains. What will you do then? Will you laugh at his downfall? No. It's all the same, me a penitent, Gregory a prisoner, what difference does any of it make? And yet – God help the man who doesn't know how to wear a mask in times like this. You think Gregory is cruel? No. Well, yes, maybe... Think of your daughter Bertha, my lady – how my feelings have changed. (*He turns on Belcredi, shouting at him*) Yes, I'll say it, I love her! Because she loved me, she stayed true when all the world had turned against me! (*He turns back to the Marchioness*) Remember, my Lady? Remember how she came with me, walking in my footsteps like a beggar, sleeping out in the open, in the snow, just to be with me? You're her mother. Don't you have any feelings? Take pity on me, for her sake, beg His Holiness to see me, beg him for forgiveness!

DONNA MATILDA (*Trembling, her voice weak*). Yes, yes, all right . . .

DOCTOR. She'll do it!

HENRY IV. Wait! (*Draws them close, confidentially*). Just seeing him won't be enough. This "Pope", as you call him, is really a sorcerer. There's nothing he can't do. He can even bring the dead back to life. (*Touching his chest*) Look what he's done to me. Can't you see? He torments me, I can't free myself, it's unbearable. (*He points fearfully at his portrait*) You can see it in him, too. I'm a penitent now, and a penitent I'll stay until he frees me. But when the excommunication is finally overturned, you two must go to the pope and beg him to release me. Release me from him (*Pointing again at his portrait*). Let me be free to live out what's left of my miserable life. I can't go on being twenty six forever. Please, my Lady, for your daughter's sake; I'll never be able to love her the way she deserves to be loved, until I'm freed from that image of myself. There. I've said all I need to say. The rest is up to you. (*Bowing*) My Lady. Monsignor.

(*He goes off, bowing grandly, through the door by which he entered. Everyone stands stunned for a moment. As his footsteps fade away the Marchioness falls to the floor, sobbing*)

ACT II

(*Another room in the villa, adjoining the throne room. Its furniture is antique and severe. Principal exit at rear in the background. To the left, two windows looking onto the garden. To the right, a door opening into the throne room.*)

Late afternoon of the same day.

*Donna Matilda, the doctor and Belcredi are in the midst of
conversation; Donna Matilda stands to one side, evidently annoyed at
what the other two are saying; although she can't help listening,
because, in her agitated state, everything interests her in spite of
herself. The talk of the other two attracts her attention, because she
instinctively feels the need for calm at the moment).*

BELCREDI. You may be right, doctor, but that was my impression.

DOCTOR. I'm not contradicting you; but, still, it's only . . . an
impression.

BELCREDI. You heard him say it with your own ears. (*Turning to the
Marchioness*). Am I right, Marchioness?

DONNA MATILDA (*Turning round*). About what? . . . (*Dubiously*).
Oh yes . . . but not for the reasons you think!

DOCTOR. He was referring to the costumes we're wearing . . . Your
cloak (*indicating the Marchioness*), our Benedictine robes . . . It's
childlike, really.

DONNA MATILDA (*Turning quickly, indignant*). Childlike? What do
you mean?

DOCTOR. From a medical standpoint – Please let me finish,
Marchioness! It's a complicated phenomenon.

DONNA MATILDA. I think it's perfectly simple!

DOCTOR (*With a smile of condescending pity*). He's insane, yes. But
madmen are still capable of observation. He knows we're playing
dress-up. But he believes in it, nonetheless. He's like a child, and for
children, reality and make-believe are indistinguishable from one
another. That's why I call it childlike. But it's complicated at the same
time, because he knows that he is both himself and his - his pretend
self (*Pointing to the portrait in the throne room*)

BELCREDI. I thought that was what he was implying.

DOCTOR. All right then – he's living in a fantasy, and we appear before him as characters from his fantasy. But his belief in his own delirium is acutely perfect, and he could tell we were only acting. So he grew suspicious. Madmen are suspicious by nature, it's part of their self-defense. To us, his condition is tragic, but from his warped perspective we're the ones engaged in some diabolical scheme. And so to draw us out, he tells us that his own disguise – which he believes is not a disguise, remember, but his *actual self* – is a joke. Make believe. Even though that's not, from his standpoint, the truth at all.

DONNA MATILDA (*Impatiently*). That can't be right!

DOCTOR. Why not?

DONNA MATILDA (*With fearful decisiveness*). He recognized me. I know it!

DOCTOR. He has no idea who you really are.

BELCREDI (*Overlapping*). He doesn't know you!

DONNA MATILDA (*More determined, almost convulsively*). I'm telling you, he knew me! When he came close to me – when he looked into my eyes -- he knew me!

BELCREDI. He was talking about your daughter!

DONNA MATILDA. No, he was talking about me!

BELCREDI. Possibly, yes, when he said . . .

DONNA MATILDA (*Losing control of her emotions*). My hair! He could see I dyed my hair! He said so!

BELCREDI. No, you're misinterpreting…

DONNA MATILDA (*Ignoring Belcredi, turning to the doctor*). I have black hair, Doctor -- like my daughter's! That's why he brought her up.

BELCREDI. He doesn't even know your daughter! He's never met her!

DONNA MATILDA. Are you that stupid? When he mentioned my daughter, he meant me! The way I used to be!

BELCREDI. I think you're coming down with his insanity!

DONNA MATILDA (*With quiet contempt*). Idiot!

BELCREDI. Were you ever his wife? No, not in his fantasy. He's married to your daughter, Bertha of Susa. Doctor, I really think she shouldn't be here...

DONNA MATILDA (*Bristling, then recovering herself. Then with a touch of anger, because she's unsure*). He was talking about me . . . he couldn't take his eyes off me, I was the only one he wanted to talk to. . .

BELCREDI. You? He delivered that whole speech to me, I couldn't keep up with him...

DONNA MATILDA (*Defiantly*). Exactly! He took an immediate dislike to you...Because he could tell that you're my lover.

DOCTOR. Not so fast, not so fast. His servants announced the Duchess Adelaide and the Bishop of Cluny, he wasn't expecting Belcredi. That's probably why he acted so suspicious.

BELCREDI. Exactly! And so he assumed I was his enemy, Peter Damiani! But she's so desperate to believe that he still has feelings for her...

DONNA MATILDA. He does, I know he does! I could see it in his eyes, doctor. A woman can always tell. It may only have been for a moment, but I could see it.

DOCTOR. He may have had a *moment* of lucidity . . .

DONNA MATILDA. Even more than a moment, Doctor. He was full of regret, for our lost youth, for the terrible accident that brought him to this place, for everything. He said so himself!

BELCREDI. Only so he could get closer to your imaginary daughter.

DOCTOR. Can I talk now? I'm a doctor, not a mind reader. I observed everything that happened, listened to everything he said. All right: his fantasy world is starting to fall apart. His adopted personality is unraveling, and now he's prone to sudden flashes of memory – *real* memories – that lead him into a reflective state of melancholy. This is good news! It shows that his mind is working again. Now, if our plan works the way we want it to...

DONNA MATILDA (*Turning to the window, in the tone of a sick person complaining*). Why isn't the car here? It's been three and a half hours.

DOCTOR. What?

DONNA MATILDA. The car, doctor! It's more than three and a half hours. . .

DOCTOR (*Taking out his watch and looking at it*). Yes, more than four hours, actually!

DONNA MATILDA. It should have been here an hour ago at least! But, as usual . . .

BELCREDI. Maybe they can't find the dress . . .

DONNA MATILDA. But I told him exactly where it was! (*Impatiently*). And Frida . . . where's Frida?

BELCREDI (*Looking out of the window*). Maybe she's in the garden with Charles . . .

DOCTOR. He'll calm her down.

BELCREDI. She's calm enough already; in fact she's bored out of her mind.

DONNA MATILDA. Don't expect much from her. I know what she's like.

DOCTOR. Anyway, it'll be over soon. It has to be tonight. We might well be able to shock him out of this, the fiction is already falling apart.

If he can be made to remember the time that's passed since his accident...

BELCREDI (*Quickly*). He'll be cured! (*Then, with emphatic irony*). We'll finally have him back!

DOCTOR. That's the hope, anyway. We'll give him a good shake like a watch that's stopped running. If only he can tell time again after being broken for so long.

(*At this point the Marquis Charles Di Nolli enters through the main entrance*).

DONNA MATILDA. Oh, Charles! . . . Where's Frida?

DI NOLLI. She's coming.

DOCTOR. Has the car arrived?

DI NOLLI. Yes.

DONNA MATILDA. They found the dress?

DI NOLLI. Yes, yes, they've got it.

DOCTOR. Good! Good!

DONNA MATILDA (*Trembling*). Where's Frida now? Where did she go?

DI NOLLI (*Shrugging his shoulders and smiling sadly, like one lending himself unwillingly to an untimely joke*). You'll see, you'll see! . . . (*Pointing towards the hall*). Here she is! . . . (*Berthold appears at the threshold of the hall, and announces with solemnity*).

BERTHOLD. Her Highness the Countess Matilda of Canossa! (*Frida enters, magnificent and beautiful, arrayed in the robes of her mother as "Countess Matilda of Tuscany," so that she is a living copy of the portrait in the throne room*).

FRIDA (*Passing Berthold, who is bowing. Disdainfully*). Of Tuscany, you moron! Canossa is just one of my castles!

BELCREDI (*In admiration*). She's like a different person . . .

DONNA MATILDA. She looks like me. Frida... you're the living image of my portrait!

DOCTOR. Yes, yes . . . She's perfect! The portrait, come to life.

BELCREDI. Beautiful!

FRIDA. Stop it! Don't make me laugh, I can hardly breathe as it is. Mother, you had such a tiny waist! I could barely fit into this.

DONNA MATILDA (*Arranging her dress a little*). Wait! . . . Hold still! . . . These pleats . . . is it really that tight on you?

FRIDA. I'm suffocating! Let's make this quick! . . .

DOCTOR. We have to wait till tonight!

FRIDA. No, no, I can't hold out that long!

DONNA MATILDA. Why did you put it on so soon?

FRIDA. It was so pretty, I couldn't resist . . .

DONNA MATILDA. You should have called me. It's so wrinkled...

FRIDA. I know, I know, but they're old wrinkles. They won't come out.

DOCTOR. It doesn't matter. The illusion is perfect. (*Placing Matilda next to her daughter*) Now, stand there . . . a little apart . . .

BELCREDI. To show the passage of time . . .

DONNA MATILDA (*slightly turning to him*). Twenty years later. And I'm a catastrophe, right?

BELCREDI. Now don't exaggerate.

DOCTOR (*Embarrassed, trying to save the situation*). No, no! I meant the dress . . . so as to see . . . You know . . .

BELCREDI (*Laughing*). It's twenty years for *us*, doctor. For him it'll be eight hundred. Do you really want to drag him across eight hundred years in a second? He'll go to pieces. (*The doctor shakes his head*) You don't think so?

DOCTOR. No, no, the human mind is stronger than you think. This world – *our* world – will become real to him again, his illusions will vanish, it'll be just like stepping down off a pedestal.

BELCREDI: I swear, doctor, I still don't understand what you want to do.

DOCTOR (*Annoyed*). You'll see! Just let me handle it . . . Now, the Marchioness is still dressed like...

BELCREDI. Wait, isn't she done acting?

DOCTOR. Soon. There's another dress waiting for her to change into as soon as he's convinced he sees the Countess Matilda of Canossa in the flesh.

FRIDA (*While talking quietly to Di Nolli notices the doctor's mistake*). Of Tuscany, of Tuscany!

DOCTOR. Whatever.

BELCREDI. Oh, I get it! He'll be confronted by two of them . . .

DOCTOR. Two, exactly! And then . . .

FRIDA (*Calling him aside*). Come here, doctor! Listen!

DOCTOR. Yes? (*Goes over to the two young people*).

BELCREDI (*Softly to Donna Matilda*). This has gone far enough.

DONNA MATILDA (*Looking him firmly in the face*). What do you mean?

BELCREDI. Why do you care what happens to him?

DONNA MATILDA. Jealous?

BELCREDI. It's not... proper. For a woman. What you're doing.

DONNA MATILDA. I owe it to him.

BELCREDI. Oh, don't be ridiculous.

DONNA MATILDA. Then why do you think I'm here?

BELCREDI. Because you know it hurts me. That's why.

DONNA MATILDA. I couldn't care less about your feelings.

DI NOLLI (*Coming forward*). All right, it's decided! (*Turning towards Berthold*): Go call one of his men.

BERTHOLD. Right away! (*Exit*).

DONNA MATILDA. So now we tell him we're going away?.

DI NOLLI. Yes, I'll take care of it . . . (*to Belcredi*) Do you mind waiting here?

BELCREDI (*Sarcastically*). Oh, no, not at all.

DI NOLLI. We don't want to arouse his suspicions.

BELCREDI. Christ, what difference does it make?!

DOCTOR. He's got to believe that we've gone away. (*Landolph followed by Berthold enters from the right*).

LANDOLPH. May I come in?

DI NOLLI. Yes, yes. Your name's Lolo, isn't it?

LANDOLPH. Lolo or Landolph, either way.

DI NOLLI. Well, listen: the doctor and the Marchioness are leaving, at once.

LANDOLPH. Hmm, all right. We'll say they obtained an audience with The Pope. The King is locked in his bedroom repenting everything he said tonight. He's desperate to receive the pardon. Would you mind talking to him just one more time? Just for a minute? In the costume, of course.

DOCTOR. I'd be glad to.

LANDOLPH. And if I could suggest... maybe add that the Marchioness of Tuscany has interceded with the Pope on his behalf?

DONNA MATILDA. You see, he recognized me!

LANDOLPH. Um... I'm not too clear on the history. Was Henry IV ever secretly in love with the Marchioness of Tuscany?

DONNA MATILDA (*At once*). No, never!

LANDOLPH. That's what I thought! But he says he loves her . . . he's always saying it . . . and that she rejected him, and now he's afraid she'll join forces with the Pope.

BELCREDI. We'll have to let him know that her feelings have changed for the better.

LANDOLPH. Yes! Right.

DONNA MATILDA (*To Belcredi*). Read your history, Belcredi. The Pope gave in to the pleading of the Marchioness Matilda and the Abbot of Cluny. And when the time's right, I intend to take advantage of that fact, to let him know my feelings were never as hostile as he thought.

BELCREDI. A slave to history, are you?

LANDOLPH. If that's the plan, why don't you just go with the Doctor and present yourself as the Marchioness of Tuscany right now?

DOCTOR (*Quickly, energetically*). No! That would spoil everything. We're looking to shake him up, remember. The Marchioness here will present herself again as the Duchess Adelaide, the mother of the Empress. And then we'll leave. That's the most important part: that he knows we've left. Come on, time's wasting! We've got a lot to do.

(*Exeunt the doctor, Donna Matilda, and Landolph, right*).

FRIDA. I'm scared.

DI NOLLI. There's nothing to be afraid of.

FRIDA. Is he violent?

DI NOLLI. No, no, gentle as a lamb.

BELCREDI (*With sarcastically sentimental affectation*). Just a hint of everyday melancholy. Didn't you hear? He's in love with you.

FRIDA. That's the part that scares me.

BELCREDI. He won't hurt you.

DI NOLLI. It'll only be a minute . . .

FRIDA. Do I have to be alone with him?

DI NOLLI. Just for a minute; we'll all be on the other side of the door, ready to burst in. Then you see your mother, you react, and your job is done.

BELCREDI. I'm afraid it's a waste of time.

DI NOLLI. Don't start that again! This might be the cure we've been looking for.

FRIDA. That's what I think. I can feel it! Feel my hand, I'm shaking!

BELCREDI. But there's one thing about His Majesty we haven't taken into account.

DI NOLLI (*Interrupting, annoyed*). What?

BELCREDI (*Forcefully*). Lunatics aren't logical!!

DI NOLLI. What's that got to do with anything?

BELCREDI. This whole scheme is so carefully thought out. So logical. The thought process he'll have to follow when he sees Frida and her mother together. But what if he doesn't react logically?

DI NOLLI. I don't think it matters. It's supposed to be a shock to his system, like the doctor said.

BELCREDI (*Suddenly*). I've never understood why psychiatrists get degrees in medicine.

FRIDA. Why?

DI NOLLI. What else would they study?

BELCREDI. Law, of course! Think about it. All psychiatrists do is talk. The more they talk, the more they seem to know. They always start by saying they can't work miracles – which somehow persuades us that a miracle will happen. Because, like lawyers…

BERTHOLD (*Who has been looking through the keyhole of the door on right*). Knock it off! They're coming!

DI NOLLI. And the King?

BERTHOLD. Yes! . . . He's coming too!

DI NOLLI. Let's clear out! (*To Berthold*) You stay here!

BERTHOLD. Do I have to?

(*Without answering him, Di Nolli, Frida, and Belcredi go out by the main exit, leaving Berthold alone. The door on the right opens, and Landolph enters first, bowing. Then Donna Matilda comes in, with mantle and ducal crown as in the first act; the doctor follows, as the abbot of Cluny. Henry IV is with them, dressed in royal robes. Ordulph and Harold enter last of all*).

HENRY IV. (*Continuing what he has been saying in the other room*). Now it's my turn to ask a question: if you think I'm so clever, why do you say I'm being stubborn?

DOCTOR. I never said that!

HENRY IV. (*Smiling, pleased*) So you approve of the way I'm handling things?

DOCTOR. I...I wouldn't say that, exactly...

HENRY IV. (*With benevolent irony*). Monsignor, in matters of politics the only options are success or failure. Either I'm a brilliant strategist or a hopeless obstructionist. Which is it? Come on now, I need the benefit of your wisdom.

DOCTOR. Do I seem wise to you?

HENRY IV. Come to think of it, no. (*Turning away to speak to Donna Matilda*). I need to speak to the Duchess. In private. (*Leads her aside and asks her very earnestly*) Do you love your daughter?

DONNA MATILDA (*Flustered*). Why, yes, of course . . .

HENRY IV. I've hurt your daughter terribly. I admit it. All right. I'm prepared to make it up to her, everything, with all the love and devotion in the world. I'm sure you've heard the rumors about my checkered past. Lies, most of it...But still...

DONNA MATILDA. No, no, I don't listen to rumors. I've never thought badly of you.

HENRY IV. So we're in agreement?

DONNA MATILDA (*Confused*). About what?

HENRY IV. That I should come back, and court your daughter again. (*Looks at her and adds, in a mysterious tone of warning*). Don't side with the Marchioness of Tuscany!

DONNA MATILDA. But I told you, she's on your side...

HENRY IV. (*Softly, but agitated*). Quiet! I won't hear it! Do you want me to lose my temper?

DONNA MATILDA (*Looks fixedly at him; then very softly as if in confidence*). You still love her, after all this time?

HENRY IV. (*Puzzled*). 'After all this time?' You know the truth, then? But nobody knows! Nobody can know!

DONNA MATILDA. But Tuscany might know, if she's been working on your behalf!

HENRY IV. (*Fixing her in his gaze*) And you say you love your daughter? (*Brief pause. He turns to the doctor; flippantly*) It's funny, I hardly ever think of my wife. Maybe it's a sin, but she's vanished from my heart. But what's even stranger, is that her own mother has so little love for her. That's right, isn't it, my Lady? You can hardly stand her. (*Turning to the Doctor*) All she talks wants to talk about is that other woman. I can't understand it!

LANDOLPH (*Humbly*). It could be, your Majesty, she thinks you misjudged the Marchioness of Tuscany. (*Embarrassed*) Just now, I mean...

HENRY IV. Are you going to defend her too?

LANDOLPH. Just this once, Your Majesty.

DONNA MATILDA. That's what I'm trying to say . . .

HENRY IV. Ah. I see. You don't think I could possibly love her. Why should you? No one has ever believed me, no one who knows me could even dream I'm capable of such a love. All well and good. (*Turning to *the doctor, his expression changing*) You see, priest? If the Pope rescinds my excommunication, it'll be for reasons that have nothing to do with why I was excommunicated in the first place. Fine. Tell the Pope we'll meet again at Brixen. As for you, Madame, should you happen to see your daughter in the course of this little intrigue, ask her to come find me. We'll see if I can finally persuade her to join me as wife and Empress. It's strange – many women have come here at night, claiming to be your daughter. But I could see the laughter in their eyes. In the bedroom – naked - one woman's just about like any other. They were all serviceable enough. But there's one woman – in one dress – her image follows me like a demon. That's what demons are, priest – not devils, not monsters from the pit, but the bedtime stories of disordered minds. The demons can come for us any time, asleep or awake, and the horror … I… I'm always afraid of my own demons. I'm afraid all the time. Even the sound of blood pulsing in my veins in the middle of the night, like distant footsteps… But enough about me. Thank you, my lady, thank you, Monsignor. (*Donna Matilda and the Doctor go off bowing. As soon as they've left, Henry IV's tone changes completely*) Idiots! They'd believe anything. And that other one – Damiani! – I saw through him immediately. He's afraid to show his face again. (*Henry IV has been pacing restlessly through the above; suddenly he sees Berthold and points him out to the other valets*) Look at him! "Duh, duh, duh", standing there like the village idiot. (*Shaking Berthold*) Are you that stupid? Can't you see, I'm the one in control now? I can say anything I want, I can make them play games and perform at my command. Pathetic, greedy clowns! (*Speaking to the other valets*) I'm sick of playing the madman! It's no fun any more. They put those disguises on to humor me, and I'll tear them off when it pleases me!

LANDOLPH -- HAROLD -- ORDULPH (*Bewildered, looking at one another*) What? I don't understand - Are you saying - ?

HENRY IV. (*Imperiously*) Enough! I'm sick to death of it! Just stop. (*Restlessly*) My god, she's shameless. Bringing her lover here to see me like this. And pretending she cares about me. Her poor, pathetic, crazy husband, locked away from the world, living out his days in a pitiful fantasy. I suppose that's why he let her do it. "Oh please, Belcredi, can't you see he needs me?" Bitch! Those people – they expect everyone to kneel down and kiss their feet, but they're not the crazy ones, oh no, no, it's just the way they think, the way they live, they way their feelings work. If you can call it feeling. And you: you just follow along, like sheep to the slaughter, you'll believe anything, do anything, your whole existence depends on it. So they tell you I'm a madman, crazy, out of my head, and you just go along. Whether you believe it or not. That's what we call "public opinion". But what about me? What about my feelings? Do you have any idea who I really am, what I go through? Listen! I'm being straight with you, for the first time. Before my accident... (*He stops suddenly, seeing their confused expressions*) What's wrong with you? (*Mockingly*) "Uh, is he crazy or not? Uh, I dunno, what do you think?" YES! I AM crazy! (*Forcing them to their knees, one by one*) Down on your knees before me! Kiss the ground at my feet! Stay down! That's how you play with a madman! (*Disgusted*) Get up. Sheep. Just sheep. You obeyed me, didn't you? Why? Because of a word, a little word. Insane. A word that weighs less than nothing, but it's crushing the life out of us all. Look, am I Henry IV? He's dead, you idiots. But you let me order you around. A dead man giving orders to the living. It's all a joke in here, isn't it? But out there – in the real world – it's not so funny. You wake up in the morning, you look at the sunrise, you say: "today I'll live for myself, today I'll start over, today is mine to make of it what I will." But you're wrong. Try as you might, you're living dead men's lives, running errands for the dead. (*To Berthold*) You don't understand a word I'm saying, do you? What's your name?

BERTHOLD. Um . . . Berthold . . .

HENRY IV. Poor Berthold! And what's your name in here?

BERTHOLD. Um... uh... Fino.

HENRY IV. Fino?

BERTHOLD. Fino Pagliuca, sire.

HENRY IV. (*Turning to Landolph*). But you use nicknames with each other, don't you? They call you Lolo.

LANDOLPH. Yes, sire . . . (*Then with a sudden sense of immense joy*). Oh, my God! He isn't crazy. . .

HENRY IV. (*Brusquely*). What?

LANDOLPH (*Hesitating*). Um... nothing . . .

HENRY IV. Not crazy, huh? No, it's a prank we're playing on all the others. (*To Harold*) -- You, your name's Franco . . . (*to Ordulph*) And yours . . .

ORDULPH. Momo.

HENRY IV. Momo, Momo . . . Perfect.

LANDOLPH. So he isn't . . .

HENRY IV. What? No, of course not! I said it was a joke, didn't I? So laugh! . . . (*Laughs*)

LANDOLPH -- HAROLD -- ORDULPH (*Looking at each other half happy and half dismayed*). He's been cured! He's all right! . . .

HENRY IV. Quiet! . . . (*To Berthold*): Why aren't you laughing? Did I upset you? Don't take anything I said personally. People have been trying to shut me up for years, don't you realize? Those people who just left – the whore, the drunk, and the swindler – they'd love for you to believe I'm insane, so you won't really listen to what I say. But they listen, and they're afraid of me. You can see it in their eyes. Why? Because I'm mad? Or because I'm not? You tell me! See? I've calmed down.

BERTHOLD. Maybe they think. . .

HENRY IV. No, no, no, look. Look me in the eyes! . . . Don't listen to my words. Words lie. Just look in my eyes.

BERTHOLD. Well . . .

HENRY IV. Can you see yourself? You're terrified. You think I've gone mad again! Then I've proved my point. (*Laughs*)

LANDOLPH (*Coming forward in the name of the others, exasperated*). What point?

HENRY IV. You're thinking, "Here we go again. He's gone crazy, again." Right? You see how easy it is to pull the rug out from under you. That's where lunatics have the advantage. You say to yourself, "It can't be. The world *has* to be logical." But for a madman, anything is possible. The world seems one way today, another way tomorrow, he drifts like a feather in the wind from one idea to another. When I was a child, I thought the moon at the bottom of the well was real. Another moon, shining out under the earth. I thought everything was real, I believed whatever I was told – and I was happy. It's only when I grew up that I learned the terrible sorrow of having to let go of yesterday's beliefs in the face of today's reality. But there's something else – something horrible – a thought that can drive sane men mad if you let yourself ponder it too long. It's that when you see yourself reflected in another's eyes, at that moment you become a beggar standing outside a locked and bolted door. The person behind that door can never be you, and you can never be him. You're both trapped in your closed-off, self-created worlds, eternally separated by that locked door we call the mind. (*Pause*) It's getting dark in here.

ORDULPH. Should I get a lamp?

HENRY IV. (*Ironically*). A lamp? . . . You turn on electric lights when I'm not around, don't you think I know that? Even in the throne room.

ORDULPH. So, should I turn on the lights?

HENRY IV. No, after all this time it would blind me! I'll stick with my oil lamp for now.

ORDULPH. I've got one ready. (*Goes to the main exit, opens the door, goes out for a moment, and returns with an ancient lamp which is held by a ring at the top*).

HENRY IV. Perfect. Sit down at the table. No, not like that. Relax. (*To Harold, posing him*) That's right (*Then to Berthold*) And you sit like this... and I'll sit here. I wish the moon was out tonight, a little moonlight makes everything look better. I spend a lot of time at my window, staring up at the moon. She knows, staring back at me, that eight hundred years have passed and I can't really be Henry IV. But still we've set up a beautiful little night scene, haven't we? An emperor surrounded by his trusty advisors. How do you like it?

LANDOLPH (*Softly to Harold, so as not to break the enchantment*). I can't believe it was all a lie! . . .

HENRY IV. What was a lie?

LANDOLPH (*Timidly, as if to excuse himself*). No . . . I mean . . . I was saying this morning to the new guy (*indicates Berthold*) -- -- I was, saying what a pity it was, that with so many nice clothes and such a fine house – and even a throne room...

HENRY IV. Yes?

LANDOLPH. Well . . . we didn't know at the time . . .

HENRY IV. That this was all a colossal joke?

LANDOLPH. Because we thought that . . .

HAROLD (*Coming to his assistance*). Yes . . . we thought you were serious!

HENRY IV. You think I'm not serious?

LANDOLPH. But you're saying. . .

HENRY IV. I'm saying you're fools! Working every day to act out *my* fantasy, instead of creating your own. This eleventh-century world could have been something that fed you, a dream you woke to every morning. You, Ordulph. (*Henry IV takes him by the arm*) Imagine what it could have been like: getting out of bed, walking into a dream, breathing it in, feeling it come to life in you. Knowing all along that it was only a dream, and feeling what a privilege it was to have no practical worries, no responsibility except to make every day a dream of beauty and excitement. Freed of the petty concerns of the modern world, no fears about what will happen tomorrow or the next day, because you'd be living inside of history, a place where tomorrow has already happened...

LANDOLPH. I get what you're saying...

HENRY IV. . . . Everything predetermined, everything settled!

ORDULPH. Yes, I see...

HENRY IV. Nothing would matter, nothing could possibly trouble you, because it's all history: my sad fate, the horrible events of this year or that year, it's all set in stone, there'd be nothing to hope for and nothing to be afraid of. No questions. In history, cause and effect is transparent, you can sit back and see how one event leads to another, no guesswork! That's the beauty of history, and that beauty, that pleasure, was all yours, if only you could have understood!

LANDOLPH. It's beautiful when you say it like that...

HENRY IV. Beautiful, yes, but it's over. Now that you know the truth, I couldn't keep it up any more. (*Taking his lamp*) Neither could you. So now I'm sick of it. (*With contained rage*) But I'll make her suffer before this is all done. Dressed up like a mother-in-law... and him as an abbot...And they brought a doctor, to experiment on me. Maybe they think I'll be cured? Idiots. And that Belcredi... I'd like to beat him senseless. They say he's a famous swordsman, maybe he'd kill me. Well, we'll see, we'll see... (*A knock at the door*) Who's there?

THE VOICE OF JOHN. Deo Gratias!

HAROLD (*Very pleased at the chance for another joke*). Oh, it's John. He's the old guy who comes every night to play the monk.

ORDULPH (*Rubbing his hands*). This should be fun!

HENRY IV. (*At once, severely*). Fun? That old man is the only one of you who dresses up out of love for me.

LANDOLPH (*to Ordulph*). So we should act like it's still true?

HENRY IV. Exactly! No jokes. (*Opens the door and admits John dressed as a humble friar with a roll of parchment under his arm*). Come in, come in, father! (*Then assuming a tone of tragic gravity and deep resentment*): Every scrap of paper that portrayed me in a good light was destroyed by my enemies. All I have left is my biography, written by this humble monk as a sign of his devotion to me. And you would laugh at him! (*Turning affectionately to John*) Sit down, father, sit down. Let's move the lamp closer to you. Now write!

JOHN (*Opens the parchment and prepares to write from dictation*). I'm ready, your Majesty!

HENRY IV. (*Dictating*). "The peace treaty proclaimed at Mayence gave hope to the poor and needy, but it threatened the interests of certain powerful factions. (*Curtain begins to fall*): It raised up the lowly, and cast down the great...

Curtain.

ACT III

The throne room is plunged in darkness. The two portraits have been taken away. Frida, dressed as the "Marchioness of Tuscany" and Charles Di Nolli, as "Henry IV" are standing where the portraits used to be.

For a moment the stage is empty. Then the door on the left opens; and Henry IV, carrying the lamp, enters. He looks back to speak to the four young men who, with John, are in the adjoining hall, as at the end of the second act.

HENRY IV. Stay where you are, I'll be fine. Good night! (*Closes the door and walks, very sad and tired, across the hall towards the second door on the right, which leads into his apartments*).

FRIDA (*Whispering from the niche, frightened*). Henry . . .

HENRY IV. (*Henry stops suddenly as if he's been stabbed in the back. Raising an arm instinctively, as if to defend himself*). Who's calling me?

It's not a question, it's a terrified exclamation, expecting no reply from the darkness and the overwhelming silence of the hall. He's suddenly consumed with fear that he might really be insane.

Frida, seeing his terror, grows terrified in turn of the part she has to play.

FRIDA (*A little more loudly*). Henry! . . .

Despite herself, Frida steps away from her assigned place and looks at DiNolli.

(*Henry cries out in terror. He lets the lamp fall from his hands to cover his face with his arms, and seems on the verge of running away*)

FRIDA (*Jumping out of the frame*). Henry! . . . Henry! . . . I'm afraid!

(*Di Nolli jumps out of his niche and runs to Frida who, on the verge of fainting, continues to cry out. The Doctor, Donna Matilda, also dressed as "Matilda of Tuscany," Belcredi, Landolph, Berthold and John enter the hall from the doors on both sides. One of them flips a light switch: hidden lamps illuminate the top half of the stage. Without paying attention to Henry, the group rush to comfort Frida. Everyone talks at the same time.*)

DI NOLLI. Frida, Frida, it's all right, I'm here!

DOCTOR (*Coming with the others*). All right, enough! Let's stop right now!

DONNA MATILDA. He's cured, Frida. Look at him!

DI NOLLI (*Astonished*). Cured?

BELCREDI. It's just a game, calm down!

FRIDA. No! I'm scared!

DONNA MATILDA. Scared of what? Look at him! He was never mad after all! . . .

DI NOLLI. That's not true! What do you mean, 'cured'?

DOCTOR. I must say, it appears that . . .

BELCREDI. Yes, yes! They told us so themselves (*Pointing to the four young men*).

DONNA MATILDA. Yes, he's been sane for a long time! He told them so himself!

DI NOLLI (*Now more indignant than surprised*). What's the meaning of this? What was he doing, then?

BELCREDI. He having a little joke on us all . . .

DI NOLLI. How is that possible? His sister went to her grave believing he was insane…

HENRY IV. (*Shouting*) That's right! Keep going!

DI NOLLI (*Startled*). Keep going? What do you mean?

HENRY IV. Your sister isn't the only one who died!

DI NOLLI. My sister? I'm talking about your sister. Who spent her last days pretending to be your mother, Agnes!

HENRY IV. So? She was *your* mother, wasn't she?

DI NOLLI. Of course she was!

HENRY IV. Whoever she was, she's been dead to me for a long time. I mourned for her in my own way, dressed in these borrowed robes.

DONNA MATILDA (*Dismayed, looking at the others*). I don't understand any of this. Keep your voice down, for Heaven's sake!

HENRY IV. What's to understand? Agnes was the mother of Henry IV, right? (*Turns to Frida as if she were really the Marchioness of Tuscany*) You ought to know, Marchioness!

FRIDA (*Still frightened, draws closer to Di Nolli*). No, no, I don't know anything!

DOCTOR. It's his mania coming back. . . Quiet now, everybody!

BELCREDI (*Indignant*). Mania, my ass! He's acting again! . . .

HENRY IV. (*Suddenly*). Me, acting? What about you?

BELCREDI. We've had enough of your games.

HENRY IV. Who said it was a game?

DOCTOR (*Loudly to Belcredi*). Don't antagonize him, for God's sake!

BELCREDI (*Raising his voice, ignoring the doctor*). They did! (*Pointing again to the four young men*) They told me it was all some sick joke!

HENRY IV. (*Turning round and looking at them*). You said it was all a joke?

LANDOLPH (*Timid and embarrassed*). No . . . not really… we said you got better.

BELCREDI. Enough! (*To Donna Matilda*) Haven't you had enough of this nonsense yet?

DONNA MATILDA. Shut up! What difference does it make if he's cured?

HENRY IV. Cured, yes! I am cured! But it's not over yet. (*Lunging at Belcredi*). For twenty years no one's had the nerve to confront me like you have.

BELCREDI. You think I don't know that? Maybe now you remember this morning...

HENRY IV. You were dressed like a monk, yes!

BELCREDI. And you thought I was Peter Damiani! It was all I could do not to laugh . . .

HENRY IV. Because you thought I was mad! And now I'm 'cured', does that strike you as funny? What do you think she looks like to me, now . . . (*interrupts himself with a gesture of contempt*) Forget it! (*Suddenly turns to the doctor*) You're a doctor, aren't you?

DOCTOR. Yes.

HENRY IV. Was all this your idea? What, a little practical joke?

DONNA MATILDA (*Impetuously*). No, no! What do you mean? We did it for your sake.

DOCTOR (*Quickly*). I was trying, in my own way…

HENRY IV. (*Cutting him short*). I understand. It was a practical joke to him (*Indicating Belcredi*) because he thinks I've been lying all along.

BELCREDI. No I don't! How could you be cured, if you were never sick to begin with?

HENRY IV. Shut up! (*To the doctor*): Do you know, doctor, that for a moment I thought I really had lost my mind? My God, to make the portraits speak; to make them jump out of their frames . . .

DOCTOR. But we all ran in as soon as we knew . . .

HENRY IV. Yes. (*Contemplates Frida and Di Nolli, and then looks at the Marchioness, and finally at his own costume*). The picture is very beautiful . . . Two couples . . . Not bad for a lunatic. (*Turning to look at Belcredi*) I'll go change into some modern clothes now. We'll go out together, you'd like that wouldn't you?

BELCREDI. Go out?

HENRY IV. Yes, let's have a night on the town. It's been too long! Where will we go? To the Club? White tie and tails? Or should we both go home with the Marchioness?

BELCREDI. Whatever you want! I have to say, it's incredible that you were able to keep this up for so long…

HENRY IV. Yes, incredible! The fact is that after I fell off that horse and hit my head, I really was out of my mind for a long time. I don't know how long.

DOCTOR. I knew it!

HENRY IV. (*Very quickly to the doctor*). Yes, doctor, I think it must have been about twelve years. (*Then suddenly turning to speak to Belcredi*): After that day I was completely unaware of how much was changing around me; how my friends deserted me, how the heart of my beloved was taken by another. How could I know, when I was dead and had simply... disappeared? It wasn't a joke for me then.

BELCREDI. That's not what I was saying. I meant later. . .

HENRY IV. Yes. Later. One day (*He stops and addresses the doctor*) – it's an interesting case, doctor. (*Trembling*) All by itself, who knows how, one day the fog lifted. Here. (*He touches his forehead*) At first I didn't know if I was asleep or awake. And then I knew I was awake. I touched one thing, then another. My eyes were opened...Oh, Jesus! Let's be done with this. Open the windows, let some air in here! Let's go out! (*Suddenly stopping himself*) But where, that's the question? Where can I show myself now? I'd be a laughing-stock.

BELCREDI. What do you mean?

DONNA MATILDA. No one blames you. It was an accident.

HENRY IV. They all said I was crazy before it happened. (*To Belcredi*): You know what I mean. You used to say so yourself.

BELCREDI. I was only kidding!

HENRY IV. Look at my grey hair! (*Shows him the hair on the nape of his neck*).

BELCREDI. My hair is grey too, now!

HENRY IV. It's different for me. I went grey when I was Henry IV, understand? And I was too far gone to notice. It all happened at once for me. I opened my eyes one day and I'd grown old, all of a sudden.

Not just on the outside, but on the inside too. Everything had fallen to pieces, all at once. My life was over, and I'd missed it.

BELCREDI. But what about everyone else?

HENRY IV. (*Quickly*). Oh yes, everyone else! All looking forward to my speedy recovery! Even the ones who betrayed me, who pricked my horse until it bled...

DI NOLLI (*Agitated*). What?

HENRY IV. Don't you know that? It was no accident. Somebody wanted my horse to rear and throw me...

DONNA MATILDA (*Quickly, in horror*). Are you serious?

HENRY IV. They probably meant it as a joke!

DONNA MATILDA. Who would do such a thing?

HENRY IV. It doesn't matter. Everyone is guilty, everyone! All of you who were so quick to leave me behind, with nothing but your pity to feed on. You know, doctor, this case must be unique in the history of insanity. I decided to *stay* insane. When I woke up everything was in place, the whole beautiful fantasy was up and running like a well-oiled machine. I decided to live inside the fantasy. That was my revenge on the world that had made me mad in the first place. I looked around at this empty house and decided to deck it out with all the color and majesty of that Carnival day twenty years ago, when you (*to Donna Matilda*) were so beautiful. I would make everyone around me keep the Carnival alive, forever. A reality, not a fantasy. Everyone dressed up, meeting me in my throne room, my four secret counselors around me. But they betrayed me. (*Turning on them*) What did you have to gain by revealing my secret? If I'm not mad, I don't need you any more! You're out of a job. Trusting people – that's the sign of a real madman. And guess what? They thought they could keep on playing this joke forever, they thought they could have a good laugh with you behind my back! (*He bursts out laughing; the others laugh along, shamefacedly – all except Donna Matilda*)

DI NOLLI (*To the four young men*). What?

HENRY IV. Forgive them. We are what we wear. I woke up to my madness, so I see now that these robes are nothing but a costume. I can put them off and be someone else. But the rest of you? You don't know the difference between who you are and what you appear to be. There's nothing to it, really. You make a solemn face, you walk around like a tragic hero (*Acting it out*) in a room like this... Here's an example, Doctor. Once I saw a priest, he must have been Irish – he was good-looking, anyway – who fell asleep on a park bench one warm, sunny November day. He was a picture of contentment, lost in his dreams, not remembering he was a priest, not thinking about where he was... A little boy wandered over with a flower in his hand. He touched the flower to the priest's neck – here, very tenderly – for just a moment. The priest awoke suddenly, but the sunlit dream still held him. His eyes were bright and laughing, there was a smile on his lips... and then, just like that, he remembered who he was and where he was. He smoothed the front of his cassock and stood. His eyes turned hard and serious – just like mine do – because he remembered suddenly that Irish priests have to defend their faith with the same single-minded zeal I devote to the cause of hereditary monarchy. Yes, I'm cured. I'm cured because I can pretend to be insane, and I can do it here, quietly, surrounded by make-believe. I feel sorry for you all. Your insanity causes you such pain and agitation, and you can't even see it.

BELCREDI. So now we're the lunatics, is that it?

HENRY IV. (*Containing his irritation*). Why else would you all have come to see me?

BELCREDI. Because I thought you were crazy.

HENRY IV. (*Suddenly indicating the Marchioness*). What about her?

BELCREDI. Who knows? She certainly seems taken with this new, conscious madness of yours. You've got the clothes for it, marchioness. Maybe you should stay here, and live out the fantasy with him.

DONNA MATILDA. Bastard!

HENRY IV. (*Conciliatingly*). No, no, he's got a point. If you were to stay, the picture would be complete, that's what he's saying. As the Marchioness of Tuscany you could never be my wife again, all you could give me was a little historical pity...

BELCREDI. More than a little! She said so herself!

HENRY IV. (*To the Marchioness, continuing*). Maybe even a little remorse...

BELCREDI. I think you could count on that.

DONNA MATILDA (*angry*). Watch your mouth . . .

HENRY IV. (*Quickly, to placate her*). Don't worry about him! He can't hurt me now. (*Turns to Belcredi*) Do you think I care what happened between you? This is my life now, not yours! You've grown old in your life, but I haven't even started to live. (*To Donna Matilda*). Was this what you wanted to show me? It was a good idea, doctor. "The past and the present together in one place". It would have worked, probably, if I'd really been mad. But I'm not mad. I know that man (*indicating DiNolli*) can't be me. I'm Henry IV, I have been these twenty years. And her? (*Indicating the Marchioness*) She's enjoyed life without me, I hardly recognize her any more. This one (*Indicating Frida*) That's the woman I remember. Are you frightened, little girl? Did they scare you with their grownup games? It's a miracle! The dream meant more to you than to anybody! It's brought you to life again! You're mine! You're mine now forever! (*He takes her in his arms, laughing maniacally. The others rush to help her*) Back! Get back! (*To the valets*) Hold them back!

(*The four young men, as if hypnotized, follow his order, and seize Di Nolli, the doctor, and Belcredi.*)

BELCREDI (*Freeing himself*). Leave her alone! Leave her alone! Stop playing!

HENRY IV. (*In one quick movement draws the sword hanging at Landolph's belt*). You think I'm playing? What about now? . . . (*Henry drives the sword into Belcredi. Everyone cries out in horror. The four men release their captives and all rush over to help Belcredi*)

DI NOLLI. Are you hurt?

BERTHOLD. Yes, yes!

DOCTOR. I told you so!

FRIDA. Oh my God! Oh my God!

DI NOLLI. Frida, come here!

DONNA MATILDA. He's out of his mind!

DI NOLLI. Hold him down!

BELCREDI (*As he's being carried out through the exit on the left*). No, no, you're not mad! You're not mad. He's not mad!

They disappear offstage. After a moment, over the clamor of voices and shouted commands offstage, we hear Donna Matilda's voice crying out in horror. Then, silence.

Henry IV is still onstage, Landolph, Harold and Ordulph standing close around him. Henry's eyes start from his head. He feels, all at once, the weight of his lifelong masquerade which has finally driven him to murder.

HENRY IV. Now... now . . . it had to be. (*Henry IV gathers his valets around him as if for protection*) We're all in this together . . . here together . . . for ever . . . for ever more.

Curtain

About the Translator

Royston Coppenger is an educator, writer and director whose work has been performed across the United States and overseas. His award-winning translations of plays by Bernard-Marie Koltès have been presented at Cucaracha Theatre, Brooklyn Academy of Music, and Cutting Ball Theater, among others. Other translations include new English versions of *Hedda Gabler* and *A Doll House* by Ibsen, *The Seagull* by Chekhov, *Playing with Fire* by August Strindberg, and *Phédre* by Jean Racine. Dr. Coppenger has taught courses in theater, film and popular culture at Harvard, New York University, and Cal Arts; he is currently Professor of Drama at Hofstra University. He holds a Doctor of Fine Arts degree in Dramaturgy and Dramatic Criticism from the Yale School of Drama.